WHAT'S THE BIG IDEA?

KNOWLEDGE and EDUCATION

Tim Cooke

Cavendish Square
New York

Published in 2018 by Cavendish Square Publishing, LLC
243 5th Avenue, Suite 136 New York, NY 10016

© 2018 Brown Bear Books Ltd

Website: cavendishsq.com

This publication represents the opinions and views of the author based on his or her personal experiences, knowledge, and research. The information in this book serves as a general guide only. The author and publisher have used their best efforts in preparing this book and disclaim liabilty rising directly or indirectly for the use and application of this book.

CPSIA compliance information: Batch #CS17CSQ.

All websites were available and accurate when this book went to press.

Library of Congress Cataloging-in-Publication Data

Names: Cooke, Tim.
Title: Knowledge and education / Tim Cooke.
Description: New York : Cavendish Square Publishing, 2018. | Series: What's the big idea?: a history of the ideas that shape our world | Includes index.
Identifiers: ISBN 9781502628183 (library bound) | ISBN 9781502628190 (ebook)
Subjects: LCSH: Education--Juvenile literature.| Philosophy--Juvenile literature.| Communication--Juvenile literature.
Classification: LCC LB1556.C365 2018 | DDC 370'.9--dc23

For Brown Bear Books Ltd:
Managing Editor: Tim Cooke
Editorial Director: Lindsey Lowe
Designer: Supriya Sahai
Design Manager: Keith Davis
Children's Publisher: Anne O'Daly
Picture Manager: Sophie Mortimer

Picture Credits:
Front Cover: Hxdbzxy/Shutterstock.com
Interior: Library of Congress: 32, 33, 35, 36-36; **Mary Evans Picture Library:** Sueddeutsche Zeitung Photo 38; **Public Domain:** 20, British Library 18-19, Castres, Bibliothéque Municipale 21, Chicago University Library 29, Christian Peacemaker Teams 23, Images of Springfield/H0n0r 34, Kalibos 27, Naple National Archaeological Museum 14, Seyyed Hossein Nasr 22; **Shutterstock:** 9, Everett Historical 39, rawpixel.com 5, Stephen Rudolph 40, Fedor Selivanov 4, Alexandre Zveiger 41; **Thinkstock:** Tony Baggett 30-31, istockphoto 8, 10, 12-13, 15, 17, Photos.com 6-7, 11, 16, 26, 28, Jan Schneckenhaus 24-25.

All other photos artwork and maps, Brown Bear Books.

Brown Bear Books has made every attempt to contact the copyright holder.
If you have any information please contact licensing@brownbearbooks.co.uk

All rights reserved. No part of this book may be reproduced, stored in a retrieval system, or transmitted in any form or by any means, electronic, mechanical, photocopying, recording, or otherwise, without the prior written permission of the copyright holder.

Manufactured in the United States of America

CONTENTS

Introduction 4
What Is Knowledge? 6
Knowledge in the Ancient World 12
Knowledge and Religions 18
The Renaissance and the Age of Reason ... 24
Growth of Education 30
The Modern Age 36
The World Today 42
Timeline 44
Glossary 46
Further Resources 47
Index 48

INTRODUCTION

Knowledge and how people pass it on from one generation to another has been an important human activity since the earliest times.

Knowledge has changed throughout history. Early societies concentrated on practical knowledge of how to find food or shelter. When they could not explain phenomena such as thunder and lightning, they guessed that these events were caused by **supernatural** forces. This began a tradition of religious or spiritual knowledge. Later, the ancient Greeks and Romans began to question the nature of the world and the purpose of life. They also began a scientific approach to acquiring knowledge, making observations, and using reason to try to explain the results.

Writing systems such as these Egyptian hieroglyphs, or picture writing, appeared about 5,000 years ago. Writing made it easier for knowledge to be passed on.

Computers and the Internet enable people to access huge amounts of information. The modern period is sometimes called the Information Age.

Religion and science

For much of history, religious and scientific knowledge co-existed. In the Middle Ages, both Christianity and Islam inspired many practical advances. In the 1500s and 1600s, however, a scientific approach became dominant. It led to a better understanding of the world and how to harness its resources. In the modern world, the sciences have become so specialized that they are only understood by experts.

Passing on knowledge

As knowledge has changed, technological breakthroughs have changed the way it is passed on. These include the invention of writing in prehistory, the printing press (ca.1440), and the World Wide Web (1989). This process was mirrored by the corresponding development of formal education. Although schooling is ancient, it was only in the late 1800s that it became mandatory for all children to receive at least some education.

WHAT IS KNOWLEDGE?

Today, children in most countries study similar subjects at school. In the past, however, there have been many ideas about what makes up knowledge.

One definition of knowledge is that it is all the facts, information, and skills we learn during our lives. Much of this knowledge is concerned with practical things, such as how to construct buildings, how to cook, or how to tie our shoes. Other knowledge concerns more **academic** information, such as the study of history, science, or geography.

CAVE ART

This bison was painted on the wall of a cave in Spain at least 14,000 years ago.

WHAT'S THE BIG IDEA?

Other knowledge is based on ideas about the meaning or purpose of life. It is closely connected to religion, which is a belief that supernatural beings or forces control the universe.

The earliest knowledge

The earliest humans learned which seeds and berries could be eaten, how to hunt animals for food, and how to make homes in caves or other natural shelters. By about 5,000 years ago, knowledge had advanced much further. People had learned to use animal skins to make clothing. They had also learned how to turn cotton and wool into thread that could be used to sew skins together or to weave cloth. People had learned to grow grains such as corn, millet, wheat, and rice.

TIMELINE

ca. 12,000 BCE — Artists paint wild animals and hand prints on the walls of a cave in Altamira, Spain.

ca. 3200 BCE — The world's first writing system develops in Sumer in Mesopotamia. Other writing systems are independently developed shortly afterward in Egypt and India.

ca. 2590 BCE — Architects in Egypt use math and engineering to build vast pyramids. Specialized workers help bring the architects' plans to reality.

They ground up the grains to make flour and bread. People had learned to clear and water the soil to grow crops. They studied the movement of the stars and planets in the sky to understand the calendar. This helped them know when it would be the best time to plant crops. They learned how to build homes and other structures from wood, stone, bricks, and other materials. People had also figured out how to dig ores from the ground and turn them into metal and how to make statues and paintings.

Knowledge and power

Some people emerged as leaders over their communities or groups of communities. They ruled kingdoms and eventually even **empires** spread over large areas. They were supported by warriors, officials, and priests. While officials learned how best to organize their lands, priests had to learn

EGYPT

Architects in ancient Egypt figured out how to design and build enormous pyramids in about 2590 BCE, after earlier attempts had collapsed.

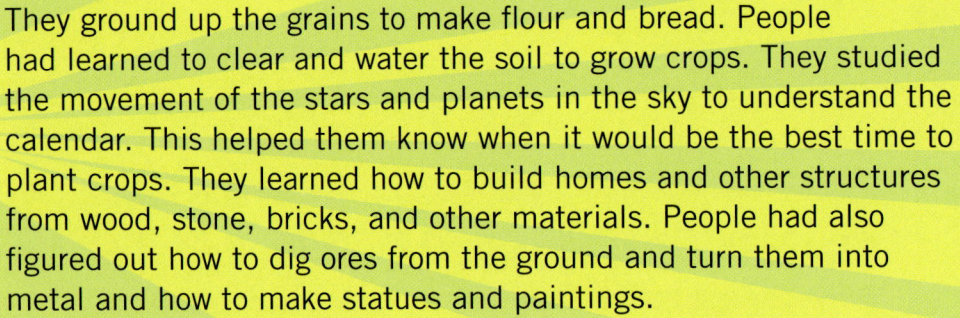

KNOWLEDGE AND EDUCATION

MESOPOTAMIA

Cities such as Babylon (*left*) on the plain between the Tigris and Euphrates Rivers controlled empires that rose to great power before declining and disappearing.

the correct **rituals** to perform in order to please the gods. Possessing this kind of special knowledge set officials and priests apart from ordinary people and helped to create an elite class.

Early societies acquired a huge amount of knowledge in places such as Egypt, India, China, Persia (modern-day Iran), and Mesopotamia (modern-day Iraq). This knowledge was passed down by word of mouth. There was no way to pass knowledge on to a wider audience. That changed in around 3200 BCE in Sumer, a kingdom in Mesopotamia. People there already used a system

INVENTION OF WRITING

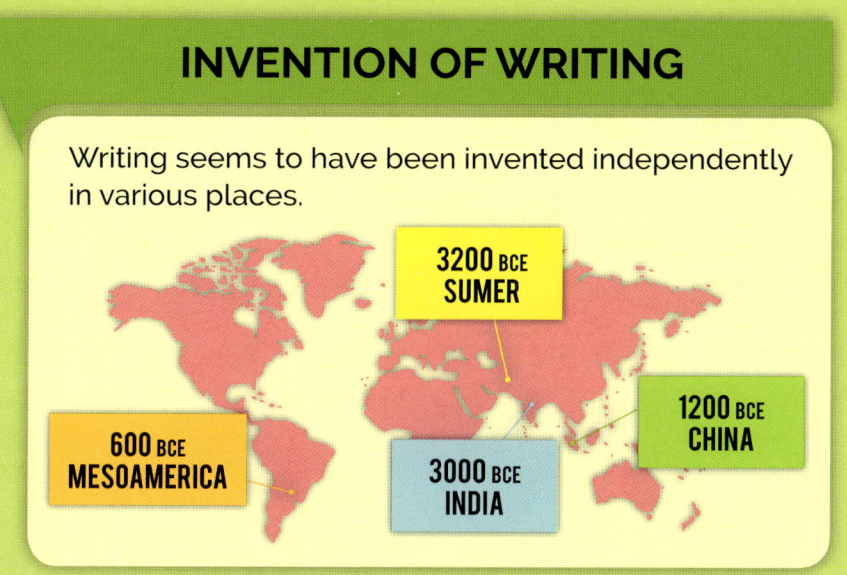

Writing seems to have been invented independently in various places.

3200 BCE SUMER

1200 BCE CHINA

600 BCE MESOAMERICA

3000 BCE INDIA

of marks in damp clay to keep records. In around 3200 BCE they created the first writing system. This was cuneiform, or "wedge-shaped" writing. It was made by pressing the end of a cut reed into clay. Cuneiform had about 1,200 separate characters. They stood for numbers, names, and objects such as cow or cloth. For centuries, cuneiform was used mainly for accounting, or recording numbers. This was important information for rulers. It told them, for example, how much tax they could collect from their subjects.

More writing develops

Soon after cuneiform appeared in Sumer, the Egyptians began to use a form of picture writing called hieroglyphics. Each character was a small picture that stood for either an object or a sound in a word. Most Egyptians could not write—even the rulers, called pharaohs, were **illiterate**. Records were kept by trained officials called **scribes**. They were among the most important people in ancient Egypt.

CUNEIFORM

Sumerian cuneiform is named for the wedge-shaped symbols pressed into soft clay using the ends of cut reeds.

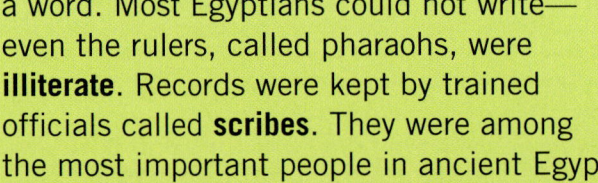

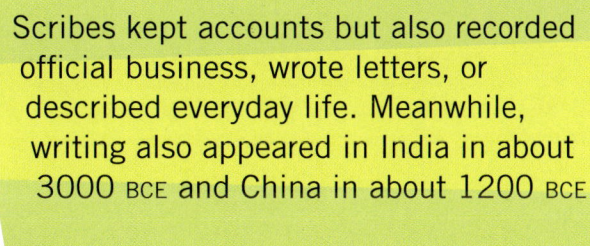

KNOWLEDGE AND EDUCATION

Scribes kept accounts but also recorded official business, wrote letters, or described everyday life. Meanwhile, writing also appeared in India in about 3000 BCE and China in about 1200 BCE.

The invention of writing enabled knowledge to be preserved and circulated more widely. As scripts evolved, writing became a more common skill. People's knowledge of the world was already considerable. The new writing systems meant that it could be stored and reused.

SCRIBE

This statue of a seated scribe was created in Egypt around 2450–2325 BCE. Scribes had great power in Egypt, where even rulers could not usually read or write.

IN SUMMARY

- Early societies acquired vast levels of knowledge about both practical and spiritual subjects.
- Possession of special knowledge helped some groups emerge as leaders of society.
- The development of writing provided a way to store, distribute, and pass on knowledge.

KNOWLEDGE IN THE ANCIENT WORLD

Writing did not change things overnight. Some of the greatest early empires had been created before writing was invented.

The greatest poet of ancient Greece, Homer, composed *The Iliad* and *The Odyssey* in around 1000 BCE, before there was any Greek writing. The **epics** were remembered by entertainers who repeated them to their audiences. Within a couple of centuries, however, the Greeks were writing down commercial records and technical **treatises**.

SOCRATES
Socrates's method of testing ideas by questioning them angered the governors of Athens so much that they forced him to kill himself.

WHAT'S THE BIG IDEA?

Ancient Greek thinkers

Meanwhile, some Greeks began to consider questions about human existence. The **philosopher** Pythagoras believed that the world was ruled by numbers and math, while Democritus suggested that all matter was made up of tiny particles called atoms. Aeschylus and Sophocles wrote popular tragedies and comedies that helped found modern theater, while in around 425 BCE Herodotus wrote the first known historical account of real events.

The greatest Greek thinkers taught in Athens. Socrates, who was born in about 470 BCE, developed a way of teaching based on questioning accepted ideas. Socrates's ideas were recorded by his follower Plato, who founded a famous academy in Athens for the study of philosophy and math. Plato's most famous pupil was Aristotle, who later taught Alexander the Great. Aristotle used **logic** to try to understand the universe and to classify knowledge into fields such as natural science, politics, and **morality**.

TIMELINE

ca. 500 BCE — The Chinese teacher Confucius argues that education and talent are more important for the government of the country than privilege and rank.

ca. 480 BCE — The city-state of Athens in Greece becomes the focus of a "golden age" of philosophy, math, natural science, and literary activity.

117 CE — The Roman Empire reaches its greatest extent. Roman settlement of Europe, North Africa, and the Middle East spreads Greek knowledge widely.

The spread of Greek knowledge

Nearly all schools in Greece were privately run. Few girls received a formal education, but most people tried to send their sons to school to learn to write. Richer students might go on to study with scholars, or sophists. The subjects included rhetoric, or public speaking, logic, geography, math, politics, and natural history. Greek thinkers introduced the idea of a set of knowledge—*paideia*—that should be taught to all male citizens. They also created a way of exploring the world using what is today called science.

Greek ideas about knowledge were inherited by the Romans in Italy. By the late 100s BCE, Rome dominated the Mediterranean, taking control of Greek lands. As Roman culture spread throughout Europe and North Africa, Greek ideas also spread.

ACADEMY

Students at Plato's academy spent their time discussing ideas. They made arguments and then tried to find weaknesses in them to see how strong the arguments were.

KNOWLEDGE AND EDUCATION

CONQUEST

The Romans spread their empire through the strength of their army. At home, however, some thinkers wondered if the state should have so much power.

The Romans also adapted Greek ideas, such as putting an emphasis on building and engineering. They built roads throughout their empire and invented the arch. The arch allowed them to build bridges, temples, and **aqueducts** to supply water to their cities.

Roman ideas

Roman scholars included the poet Lucretius and the lawyer Cicero. Cicero's skill as an orator, or public speaker, made him an influential politician in Rome.

GREEK INFLUENCE

Greek thinkers helped establish many modern areas of study:

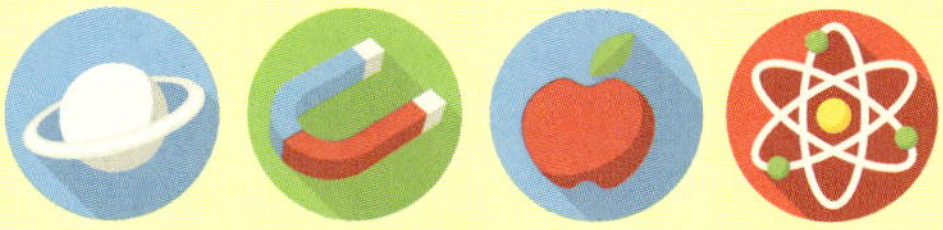

ZOOLOGY	Aristotle
BOTANY	Theophrastus
MATH	Pythagoras
CARTOGRAPHY	Anaximander
ASTRONOMY	Ptolemy
ELECTRICITY AND MAGNETISM	Thales of Miletus
ATOMIC SCIENCE	Democritus

Cicero spent much of his time trying to figure out how laws could be made to restrain the power of Rome's rulers, whom he believed were too powerful. Another scholar, Tacitus, agreed with Cicero. In his history of the Roman empire, he looked forward to a time "when we may think what we please, and express what we think."

Roman boys and girls were usually educated separately, and children of different ages went to different schools. Often only the richest families could afford to send their children to the most advanced schools. It is estimated that the number of people who could read rose from 5 percent in ancient Greece to a little over 10 percent in the Roman empire.

Developments in Asia

Meanwhile, in Asia knowledge and education were heavily influenced by religion. In India, long poems called the Vedas passed on the stories on which the Hindu religion was based. In the 500s BCE, the teachings

CICERO

Cicero's ideas about public affairs and what made people suitable for government influenced European thought over 1,000 years later in the Renaissance.

KNOWLEDGE AND EDUCATION

of an Indian prophet known as the Buddha were also being carried throughout South and East Asia. What Buddha had said had been written down by his followers. It was widely copied and carried to other lands.

In China, meanwhile, a sixth-century-BCE scholar named Confucius had begun an influential approach to knowledge known as Confucianism. Confucius taught that morality and learning were a great benefit to the Chinese state. His teachings became the basis of demanding examinations for students who wanted to work in the Chinese civil service.

CONFUCIUS

According to Confucius, the key to learning was experience. He taught that younger people should respect their elders, who were also their teachers.

IN SUMMARY

- Around the world, writing allowed scholars to record their thoughts about the surrounding environment, and helped their theories to spread.

- Ideas from ancient Greece were spread by the Romans and became influential over a large region, particularly in Europe and the Middle East.

Knowledge and Religions

During the Middle Ages (ca. 500–1500 CE), one of the most important influences on education came from religion.

At the start of the first century, Christianity had begun in what is now Israel and Palestine. Stories of the life of a teacher named Jesus were written down in the late first century in what became the New Testament of the Christian Bible. The Romans executed Jesus in around 33 CE, but preachers spread his teachings around the Roman world. Despite being attacked, the faith gained more and more followers.

SCHOLAR

In the 1200s, the French Dominican monk Vincent of Beauvais wrote an encyclopedia that was widely used for centuries.

WHAT'S THE BIG IDEA?

The divided Roman Empire

In 285 CE, the Roman Empire split into western and eastern empires. In 380, Christianity became the official religion of the Roman Empire in the West, and Rome became the headquarters of the Catholic Church. Early Christian thinkers such as St. Augustine and Boethius were concerned to show that it was possible to prove faith in God by logical argument, an approach known as scholasticism. Meanwhile, monks and nuns lived in communities in monasteries and convents, where they spent their time studying God's word. They copied religious texts by hand.

In 476, the Roman Empire in the West was overthrown by a Germanic people. The Eastern Empire survived until 1453, but was known as the Byzantine Empire. For centuries after the fall of Rome, Europe went into a decline.

TIMELINE

476 — Rome is overthrown by Germanic peoples, beginning a decline that later ages will call the Dark Ages.

800 — Charlemagne becomes Holy Roman Emperor. He encourages scholarship by setting up a school in Aachen. Learning is international because it is done in Latin, the language of ancient Rome.

ca. 1200 — Texts by classical writers such as Plato and Aristotle begin to reach Europe via the Islamic Middle East, where they have been preserved.

There was less trade, cities were abandoned, and roads and buildings crumbled. The institutions of government grew weaker, and **classical** knowledge was largely forgotten. Learning did not come to an end, however. Although people later called this period the Dark Ages, it was actually a time of growing education.

Monastery schools in Europe

Most schools were run by monasteries and convents. They prepared pupils to take holy orders, meaning they would become priests or nuns. Students learned to write and memorized Latin phrases by chanting them out loud. In the 800s, King Charlemagne of the Franks established an empire in central Europe. He invited scholars from around the continent to a school he founded in his capital at Aachen. When those scholars returned home, they set up monastic schools in France, Germany, and Italy. Later in the century, the English king Alfred the Great

WRITING

King Charlemagne's scholars developed a way of writing that is close to how we write today. It is known as Carolingian minuscule.

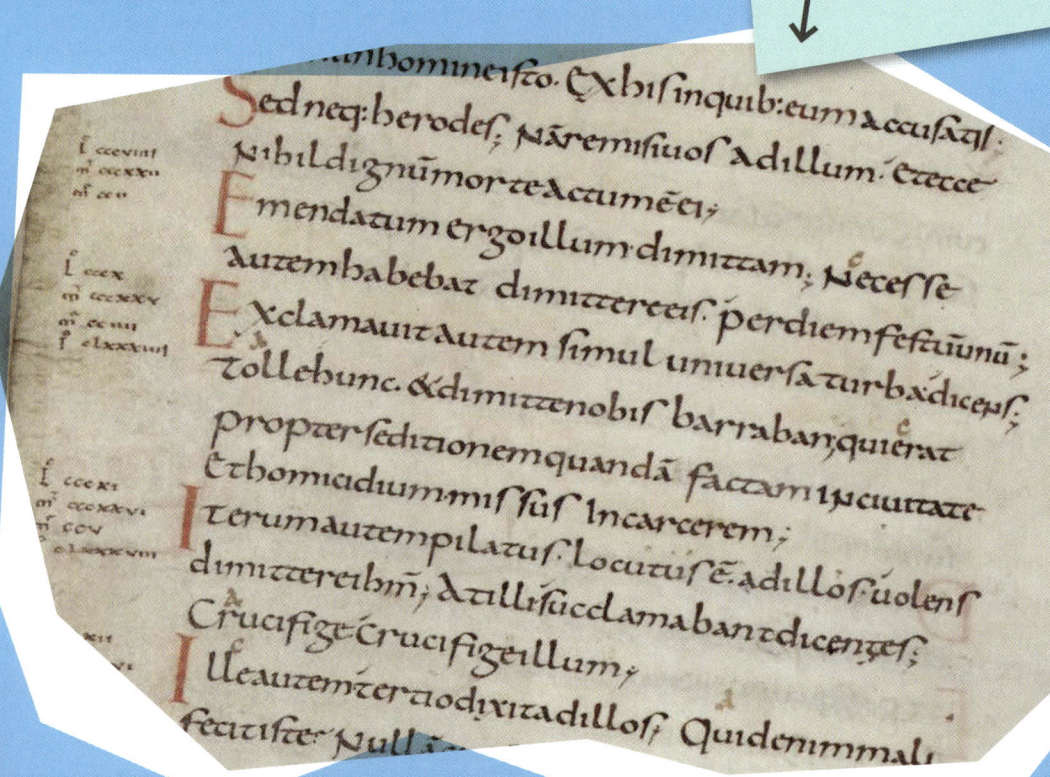

KNOWLEDGE AND EDUCATION

MONASTERY SCHOOL

A monk reads to his students. Although one pupil has a book, books were very rare. Most learning was done by memorizing passages by repeating them out loud.

invited European monks to England in order to teach Latin to students and to translate Latin texts into English.

The growth of towns

From the 1000s, towns grew in Western Europe. Their citizens wanted their children to be educated. By the late 1100s, cathedrals and merchant groups ran schools in towns in Germany, Italy, and the Netherlands. All pupils studied the same **curriculum**, which had two parts, the trivium and the quadrivium.

THE CURRICULUM

The curriculum at cathedral schools was in two parts. Everyone studied the trivium. Smarter children then studied the quadrivium.

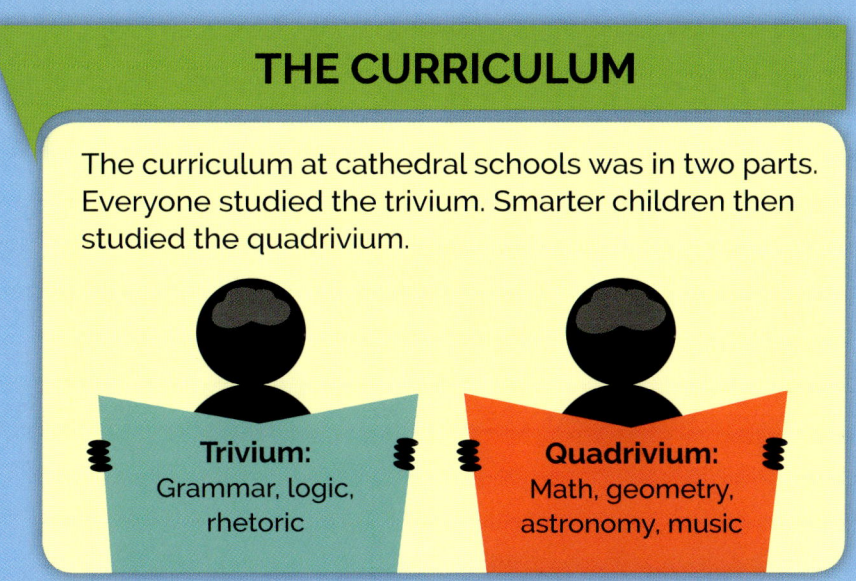

Trivium: Grammar, logic, rhetoric

Quadrivium: Math, geometry, astronomy, music

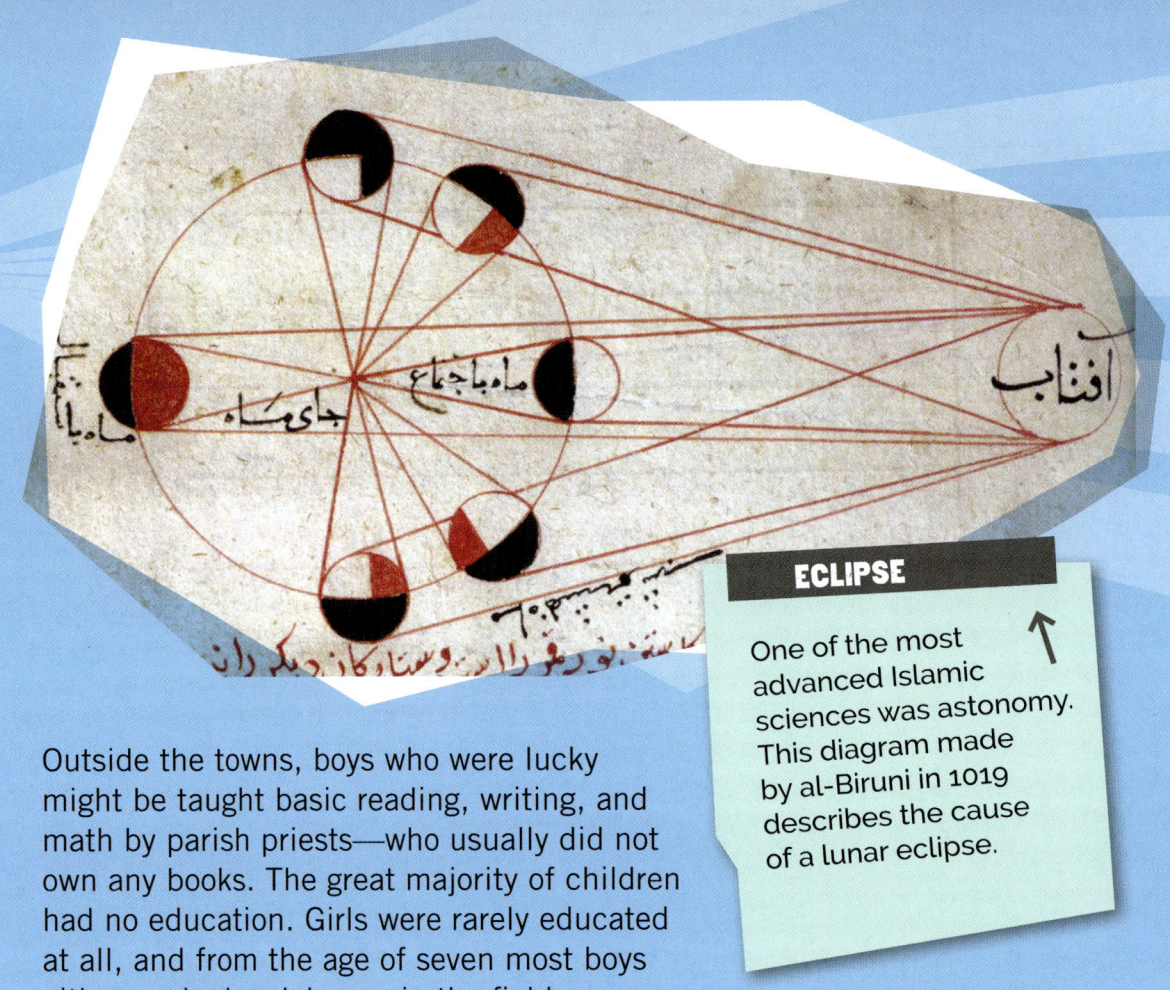

ECLIPSE
One of the most advanced Islamic sciences was astonomy. This diagram made by al-Biruni in 1019 describes the cause of a lunar eclipse.

Outside the towns, boys who were lucky might be taught basic reading, writing, and math by parish priests—who usually did not own any books. The great majority of children had no education. Girls were rarely educated at all, and from the age of seven most boys either worked as laborers in the fields or became apprenticed to older craftsmen. Apprentices spent years working for their masters while they learned practical knowledge from them. Meanwhile, **literacy** rates in the Byzantine Empire were higher than in Western Europe, because the Byzantines set up schools for six- to ten-year-old boys.

Islam and learning
Christianity was not the only religion that encouraged education and literacy. In the middle of the 600s the prophet Muhammad founded Islam in Arabia. The new faith spread swiftly throughout the Middle East, Central Asia, and North Africa. Islamic countries stretched from Spain in the west to India in the east. Education was key to Islam. Students and scholars gathered at mosques to discuss the Quran, the sacred book of Islam.

KNOWLEDGE AND EDUCATION

MADRASAH

Al-Mustansiriya University in Baghdad, Iraq, was founded as a madrasah in 1227. It is one of the oldest universities in the world.

Boys went to elementary school to learn to read or write, to do math, and to memorize the Quran. As they grew older, smarter students also studied oratory, history, and ethics.

A new type of school emerged to train men as government officials or priests. These madrasahs taught religion and the physical sciences. They were responsible for a huge advance in learning. Students dissected animals, discovered new drugs, and observed the stars. They also studied classical works by scholars such as Aristotle. It was through the work of Islamic scholars that people in the West first became familiar with classical works from about 1200 onward.

IN SUMMARY

- After the fall of the Roman Empire, learning was continued in monasteries and convents.
- Monks provided schooling for future priests and for the sons of merchants in the growing towns.
- Islam encouraged literacy in madrasahs, and Islamic scholars made advances in many subjects.

THE RENAISSANCE AND THE AGE OF REASON

Medieval education prepared pupils for the church. The Renaissance brought a new attitude toward learning.

The Renaissance was a period of great advances in learning and the arts. It began in Europe in about 1300 and lasted until about 1650. From classical texts, which had often been preserved in Islamic countries, scholars developed what was called humanism. Humanism was a way of thinking that focused on the role of the individual in society. In 1402 an Italian humanist named Pietro Paolo Vergerio

PRINTING PRESS

Johannes Gutenberg's invention led to a huge increase in the number of books printed in Europe from the 1440s onward.

WHAT'S THE BIG IDEA?

argued that math, astronomy, and the natural sciences helped people to understand their place in the world. He said the subjects would liberate people's potential. These subjects became known as the liberal arts.

The spread of humanism

During the 1400s, a type of secondary school called a gymnasium emerged in Italian cities such as Padua, Verona, Mantua, and Venice. Students learned **grammar** and rhetoric, or the art of public speaking. They also studied the liberal arts, medicine, law, and theology. There was an emphasis on Latin and Greek, but also on physical education. The schools tried to produce students who were both smart and fit.

Many Italian rulers and their courtiers came to see education as an essential part of being a civilized person. Tutors were employed to teach at the courts of Italy, which became centers of humanism.

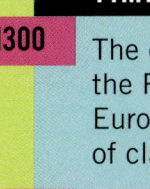

TIMELINE

ca. 1300 — The cultural movement known as the Renaissance begins in Europe. Europeans see the period as a rebirth of classical knowledge.

ca. 1440 — In Germany, Johannes Gutenberg invents a printing press with reusable type, making it possible to print books more quickly and cheaply than before.

1517 — The authority of the Catholic Church is challenged in the Reformation by Protestant reformers who emphasize the importance of people reading the Bible for themselves.

The influence of humanism spread widely. It spread partly through books. The invention of the printing press by Johannes Gutenberg in Germany in the 1440s made books more widely available. Humanism also spread through education. In England, humanist ideas led to the creation of schools that concentrated on teaching grammar. These grammar schools remained a model of education for centuries. Between 1500 and 1620, more than 300 grammar schools were set up in England. The creation of schools was also encouraged by the Protestant Reformation that began in 1517. Followers of Protestantism argued that everyone should be able to read the Bible for themselves.

International knowledge

Meanwhile, the first universities had appeared in Italy in the 1000s, followed by France, Germany, and England. Most university courses focused on **professional** skills, such as law or medicine, or on the liberal arts. Students traveled widely throughout Europe. Ideas that began in the universities therefore spread across the continent.

ERASMUS

The Dutch humanist Erasmus spent much of his life in England, where he encouraged the development of grammar schools.

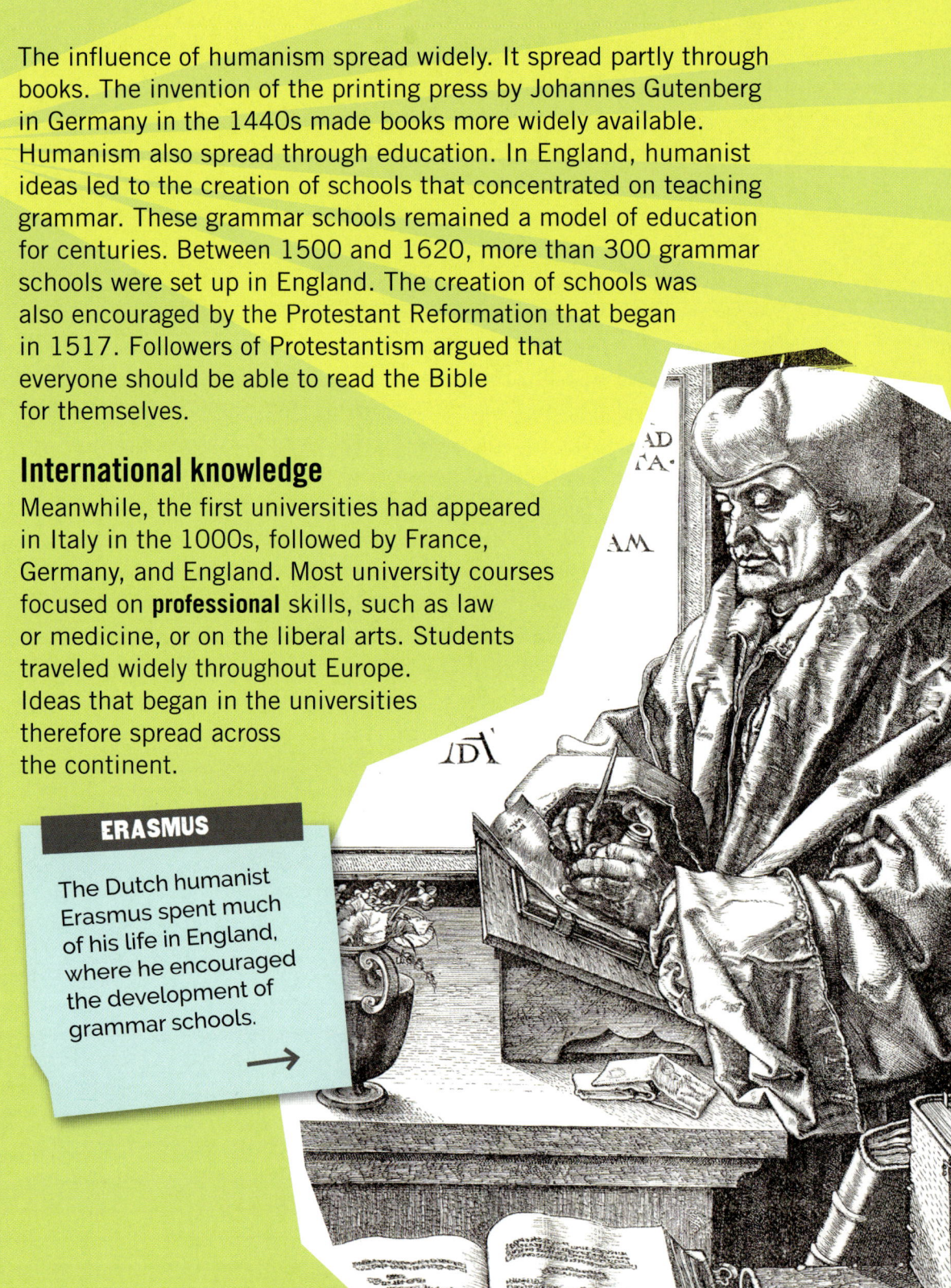

KNOWLEDGE AND EDUCATION

UNIVERSITY

← This lecture theater in Padua University, Italy, was used for public dissections of dead bodies so that students could learn about human anatomy.

By the late 1600s, literacy levels were quite high in Europe's towns. It was important for many people to know some reading, writing, and math in order to run their businesses. Many Protestants learned to read as part of their faith. In the countryside, by contrast, peasant children working in the fields had little need of formal education. Some boys were taught to read by the village priest, but girls received little or no education, apart from in household skills.

FIRST UNIVERSITIES

A university was founded in Cairo in Egypt in 970. The movement spread throughout Europe over the following century.

1088 Bologna, Italy
1134 Salamanca, Spain
1150 Paris, France
1167 Oxford, England
1209 Cambridge, England
1222 Padua, Italy

27

Ideas about knowledge were changing. During the Renaissance, **astonomers** such as Nicolaus Copernicus from Poland and Galileo Galilei from Italy established new laws about the universe. Copernicus thought that the Earth orbited the Sun. He clashed with the Catholic Church, which taught that Earth was the center of the universe. Galileo used a new invention, the telescope, to observe the heavens. The evidence he gathered supported Copernicus' **theory**. In England, Isaac Newton proposed three laws of motion and a law of gravity. Together, the rules explained why all objects in the universe move. Newton also investigated other subjects, including the nature of light and astronomy.

The Scientific Revolution

Across Europe, men such as Johannes Kepler, René Descartes, Christiaan Huygens, and Robert Boyle were making fundamental discoveries. They founded many branches of

COPERNICUS

This diagram reflects Copernicus's theory that earth orbits the sun. The heliocentric, or sun-centered, universe directly went against the ideas of the Catholic Church.

KNOWLEDGE AND EDUCATION

modern study, including **chemistry**. Their method was based on experiment and observation rather than on ancient classical texts or religious beliefs.

The period from about 1550 to 1700 is sometimes known as the Scientific Revolution or the Age of Reason. It saw the emergence of a methodical approach to acquiring knowledge. There was a growth of interest in classifying plants and animals, and academies, societies, and museums opened across Europe to promote scientific study.

The new scientific approach to knowledge was summed up in an encyclopedia compiled in France by Denis Diderot from 1751 to 1772. The *Encyclopédie* aimed to classify all of human knowledge, both practical and philosophical. Diderot said it would "change the way people think."

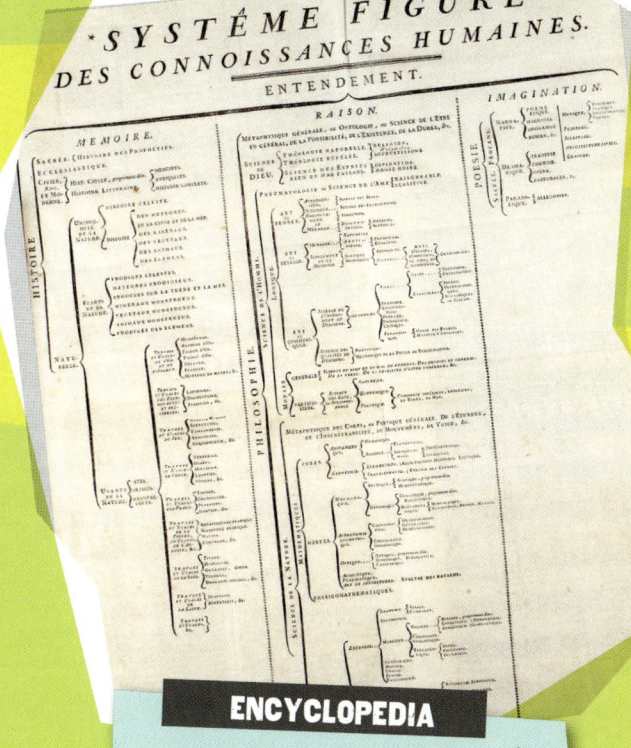

ENCYCLOPEDIA

Diderot's *Encyclopédie* was based on classifying all human knowledge into different logical sections, as laid out here at the start of the work.

IN SUMMARY

- The Renaissance idea of humanism encouraged the spread of education based on classical ideas.
- Protestants argued that everyone should read the Bible for him or herself.
- Thinkers began to use reason and observation to question the ideas of the Catholic Church.

GROWTH OF EDUCATION

During the 1800s, formal schooling became standard in most of the world's leading countries.

In the French Revolution (1789–1799), citizens in Europe overthrew their rulers for the first time. During the 1800s, many other rulers in Europe reacted to popular pressure by allowing at least some of their citizens to vote in elections. This change was matched by dramatic changes in technology. The invention of the steam engine in the late 1700s began the Industrial Revolution. Activities such as weaving became dominated by machines. Many workers did unskilled factory jobs in overcrowded towns and cities.

WHAT'S THE BIG IDEA?

A growing need

In the late 1700s, the changing world convinced many observers that countries needed to start educating their citizens. Social reformers believed that education could help defeat the evils of poverty. Other people thought that people who could vote should be able to read about political issues. However, when Prussia in Germany introduced mass schooling in around 1800, its aim was to create better recruits for its army rather than simply to educate its citizens. The Prussian system was introduced to France in the 1830s.

PUNISHMENT

British students were caned on the hand as a punishment for poor behavior. Physical punishment was common in schools in the 1800s.

TIMELINE

1790s — Noah Webster publishes *The American Spelling Book*, which teaches children to read while also trying to give them basic lessons about citizenship.

1800 — Prussia, a state in what is now Germany, introduces mass schooling to try to improve the quality of its army.

1880 — Britain makes elementary schooling mandatory for all children aged between five and ten years.

Britain's school system

In Britain, Robert Raikes had begun a system of **Sunday schools** in 1780. The schools taught boys from the slums to read. By the early 1830s, 1.25 million British children were going to Sunday school, and the government began to build schools in England and Wales. In Scotland, universal education had begun in the 1600s as part of the Reformation. By the 1860s, 90 percent of British children went to elementary school. In 1880 schooling became mandatory for children aged from five to ten years. The age at which pupils could leave school was raised over the following decades. A similar process took place in most Western countries and their **colonies**.

In the 1800s, most British schools taught what were known as the "Three Rs"—reading, 'riting, and 'rithmetic (math). Grammar schools concentrated on classical languages and literature. In the early 1900s a new type of school appeared. It taught technical skills to students who had more talent for practical rather than academic subjects.

CLASSROOM

Young schoolboys pose at their desks in Berlin, Germany, in the late 1800s. It was common for boys and girls to be taught in separate classes or even in separate schools.

KNOWLEDGE AND EDUCATION

WEBSTER
Noah Webster believed that literacy was vital to the prosperity of the United States. He wrote an important spelling book and the first American dictionary.

The United States

In America, schooling had been important before independence in 1776. American churches urged worshipers to learn to read the Bible. Two important textbooks appeared in the 1790s. The *New England Primer* taught pupils to read by using verses with a religious message. Noah Webster's *American Speller*, meanwhile, contained messages about civics. Students learned letters before moving on to short words, longer words, then sentences. Webster hoped his book would help create good citizens for the republic.

LITERACY IN 1900

Literacy rates rose in the United States throughout the 1800s, although they remained low among African Americans and minority populations.

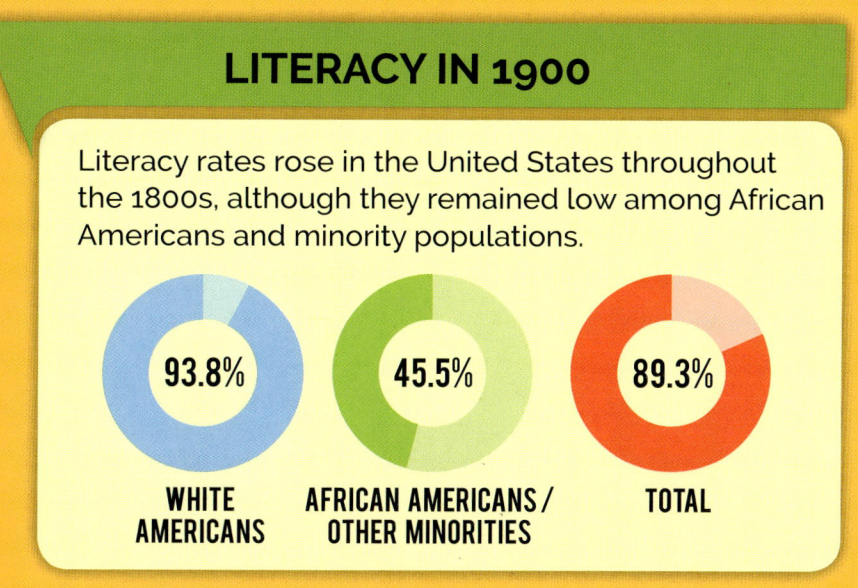

93.8% WHITE AMERICANS

45.5% AFRICAN AMERICANS / OTHER MINORITIES

89.3% TOTAL

In the late 1800s many states opened free elementary schools alongside the fee-paying academies in larger cities. Most followed a system set up by Horace Mann in Massachusetts. In Mann's system, all schools taught the same curriculum and students were split into grades based on age. In the Midwest and West, meanwhile, schools often only had one room and a single teacher. By 1900 around three-quarters of American children went to school. By 1918, elementary education was mandatory in every state. In the early 1900s, secondary, or high-school, education also became mandatory throughout the United States and Europe.

African American schools

The black activist Booker T. Washington argued that education was vital for African Americans. **Segregated** black schools taught industrial and technical skills. Washington argued that they should also teach professional subjects in order to help African Americans improve their lives.

SCHOOL HOUSE

In one-room schools in the American West and Midwest, older students assisted the teacher by helping the younger students with reading and math.

KNOWLEDGE AND EDUCATION

FEMALE STUDENTS
This photograph shows girls at Washington, DC, High School in 1886. Many high schools had exams that restricted entry to a small part of the population.

Significant advances
Alongside the growth of education, the 1800s saw huge advances in the world's knowledge. This was also the time when knowledge began to fracture into specialized branches. Scientists introduced gas lighting, followed by electric lighting. Inventors developed labor-saving appliances, synthetic dyes, and the bicycle. Among the most significant breakthroughs were those of Michael Faraday and Charles Darwin. Faraday learned how to generate electricity. Darwin's theory of how species evolved through evolution, published in 1859, caused a sensation. It contradicted the biblical account of how humans were created.

IN SUMMARY
- The growth of schooling was a result of the growth of democracy, industrialization, and social reform.
- Literacy levels grew as school attendance rose throughout the 1800s.
- By the early 1900s, mandatory schooling was common in most Western nations.

The Modern Age

Since 1900, there have been major changes in how people see knowledge.

In the early 1900s, artists, writers, and musicians began trying to make their work more closely reflect the changing world around them. They created modern forms of thought and expression. These forms included abstraction, or paintings that did not portray things, and music that was often considered to be tuneless.

ALBERT EINSTEIN

German-born Einstein became a US citizen after moving to North America to escape Nazi Germany.

WHAT'S THE BIG IDEA?

Theory and practice

Meanwhile, scientists such as Albert Einstein from Germany also questioned accepted scientific laws. In the 1680s, Isaac Newton had explained that gravity was a force caused by an object's mass. In 1916, Einstein argued instead that gravity arises from the fact that space and time are curved.

Einstein and other physicists studied **theoretical** forces and particles. Although their work could not be understood by most people, it was the basis of many practical advances. The theories led to a revolution in communications with the invention of the radio, the telephone, and the television. The radio and the television became hugely powerful in bringing information into the home. Mass-circulation newspapers and magazines were also a major source of information and advertising by corporations and retailers.

TIMELINE

1916	Albert Einstein publishes his theory of general relativity, a work that symbolizes the emergence of a new kind of science.
1945	The atom bomb, developed by a team of American and European physicists, is dropped on Japanese cities, ushering in the end of World War II.
1989	British scientist Tim Berners-Lee first proposes the World Wide Web, in which information becomes easily shared by people who have computers.

Knowledge through warfare

In the 1930s, Einstein and other academics moved to Britain and North America. As a result, the United States became one the world's leading academic powers. Many of these exiles were Jews fleeing the Nazi dictator Adolf Hitler, who took power in Germany in 1933. Hitler used the German education system to train children to become unquestioning Nazis. He convinced many Germans of a false interpretation of history that blamed Jews for a series of problems. In Japan, meanwhile, a **nationalistic** government also used education to create a highly disciplined, militaristic culture.

In 1939, Hitler's desire to control more territory led to World War II (1939–1945). Just as had happened in World War I (1914–1918), the war increased the speed of technological development. In World War I, the submarine, the tank, and poison gas were developed. In World War II, the Germans developed fighter jets and rockets, while the **Allies** invented radar and used the first computer to crack German codes. The ultimate demonstration of Allied technological superiority came with the creation of the atomic bomb.

PROPAGANDA

The Nazi leader Adolf Hitler used the education system to persuade young Germans to accept his inaccurate version of history.

KNOWLEDGE AND EDUCATION

ATOM BOMB

On August 6, 1945, a US airplane dropped an atom bomb that destroyed the Japanese city of Hiroshima. The world had entered the atomic age.

Created by a team that included many European exiles, the weapon used the potential energy generated by splitting atoms or smashing them together to generate huge destructive force.

Another wartime advance came in medical knowledge. In 1928, the Scot Alexander Fleming found a mold that killed **bacteria**. The discovery led to the creation of penicillin. This first antibiotic improved the survival rate of wounded soldiers in World War II.

GROWTH OF THE WORLD WIDE WEB

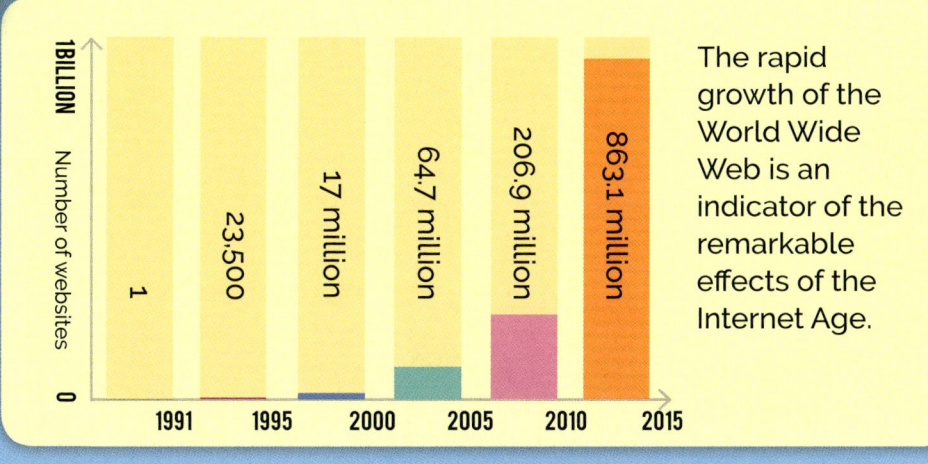

Year	Number of websites
1991	1
1995	23,500
2000	17 million
2005	64.7 million
2010	206.9 million
2015	863.1 million

The rapid growth of the World Wide Web is an indicator of the remarkable effects of the Internet Age.

COMPUTER

The first computers were built in the 1950s and 1960s, but personal computers (PCs) only became common from the late 1980s onward.

The space age

Numerous advances in knowledge following World War II would change the lives of ordinary people. In 1953, researchers in Britain discovered DNA, the material that carries hereditary information from parents to their offspring. That suggested that genetic engineering might one day be able to reduce inherited diseases. Color TV was introduced, and microwave ovens were among a new generation of kitchen appliances.

Meanwhile, in the late 1950s, a race began between US and Soviet scientists to claim control of space. The space race led to the development of satellites to help with communications. The US space program focused on putting a man on the Moon. On July 16, 1969, *Apollo 11* landed on the Moon. The Apollo program also drove numerous other technological advances.

The computer age

The biggest advance, however, came with the emergence of computers. The rise of computing was boosted by the linking of computers via the Internet in the 1960s, and in the 1980s by the World Wide Web. Invented by British scientist Tim Berners-Lee, the Web allowed people to share information. The invention sparked the creation of millions of websites, ranging from the frivolous to the highly academic.

Over the following decades, a series of further developments—video and music streaming, social media, wireless technology, the Cloud—revolutionized the way knowledge is stored and distributed. By placing an emphasis on individuals rather than organizations, and by giving non-experts a larger role in the exchange of information, such developments may have also changed the nature of knowledge itself.

TABLET

Tablets and smartphones now make it possible to access the World Wide Web from virtually anywhere in the world.

IN SUMMARY

- Knowledge grew more rapidly during the 20th century than at any time in history.
- Much technological change was driven by two world wars and the Cold War.
- The computer and the Internet changed the nature and distribution of knowledge forever.

THE WORLD TODAY

Today, knowledge is best judged by looking at levels of literacy, higher education, and access to computers and the Internet.

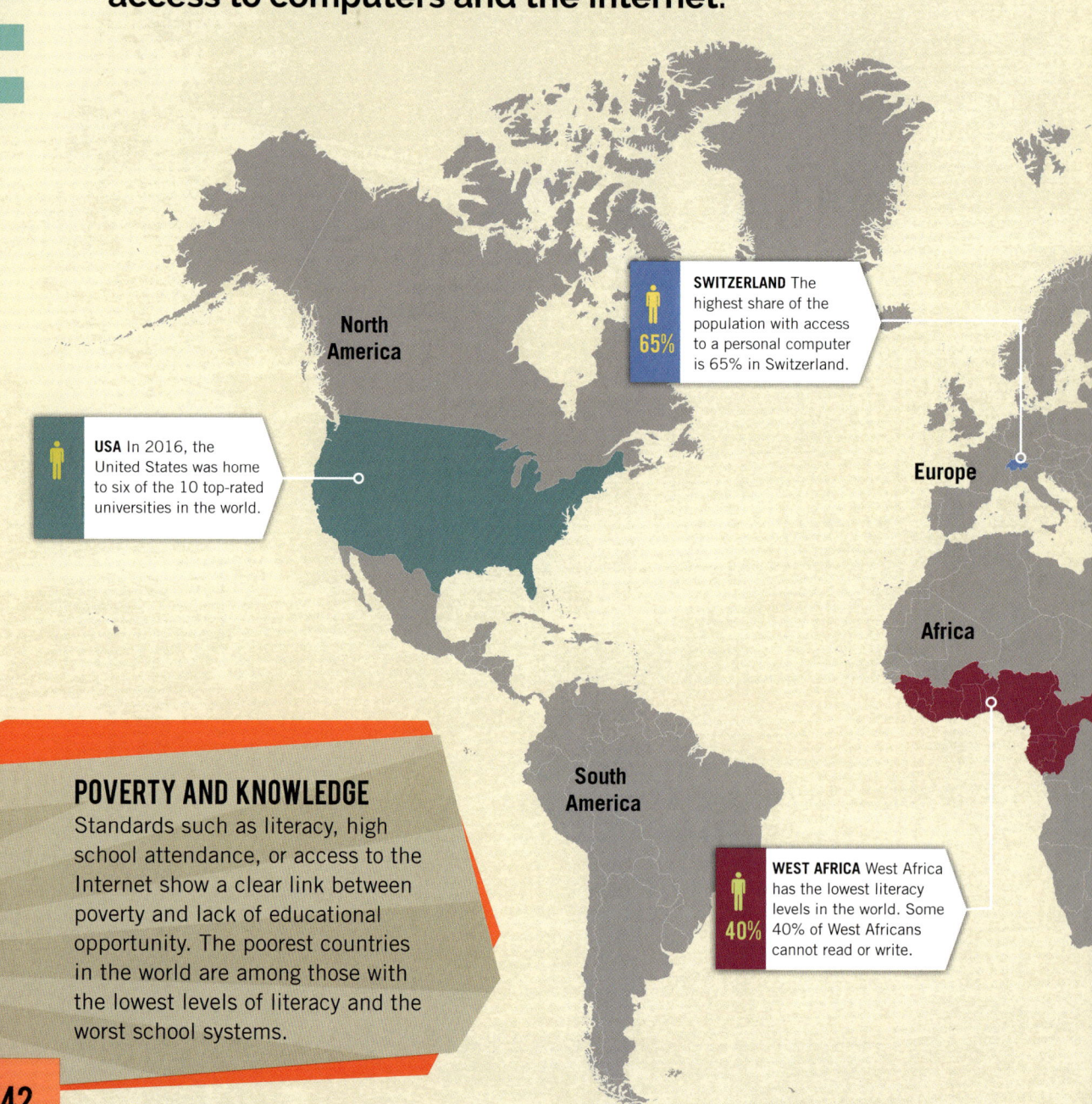

SWITZERLAND The highest share of the population with access to a personal computer is 65% in Switzerland.

USA In 2016, the United States was home to six of the 10 top-rated universities in the world.

WEST AFRICA West Africa has the lowest literacy levels in the world. Some 40% of West Africans cannot read or write.

POVERTY AND KNOWLEDGE

Standards such as literacy, high school attendance, or access to the Internet show a clear link between poverty and lack of educational opportunity. The poorest countries in the world are among those with the lowest levels of literacy and the worst school systems.

PUBLIC LIBRARIES

Libraries where the public can read books and periodicals free of charge opened in Europe and North America in the late 1800s. The countries with most public libraries in 2016 were China, Russia, and India.

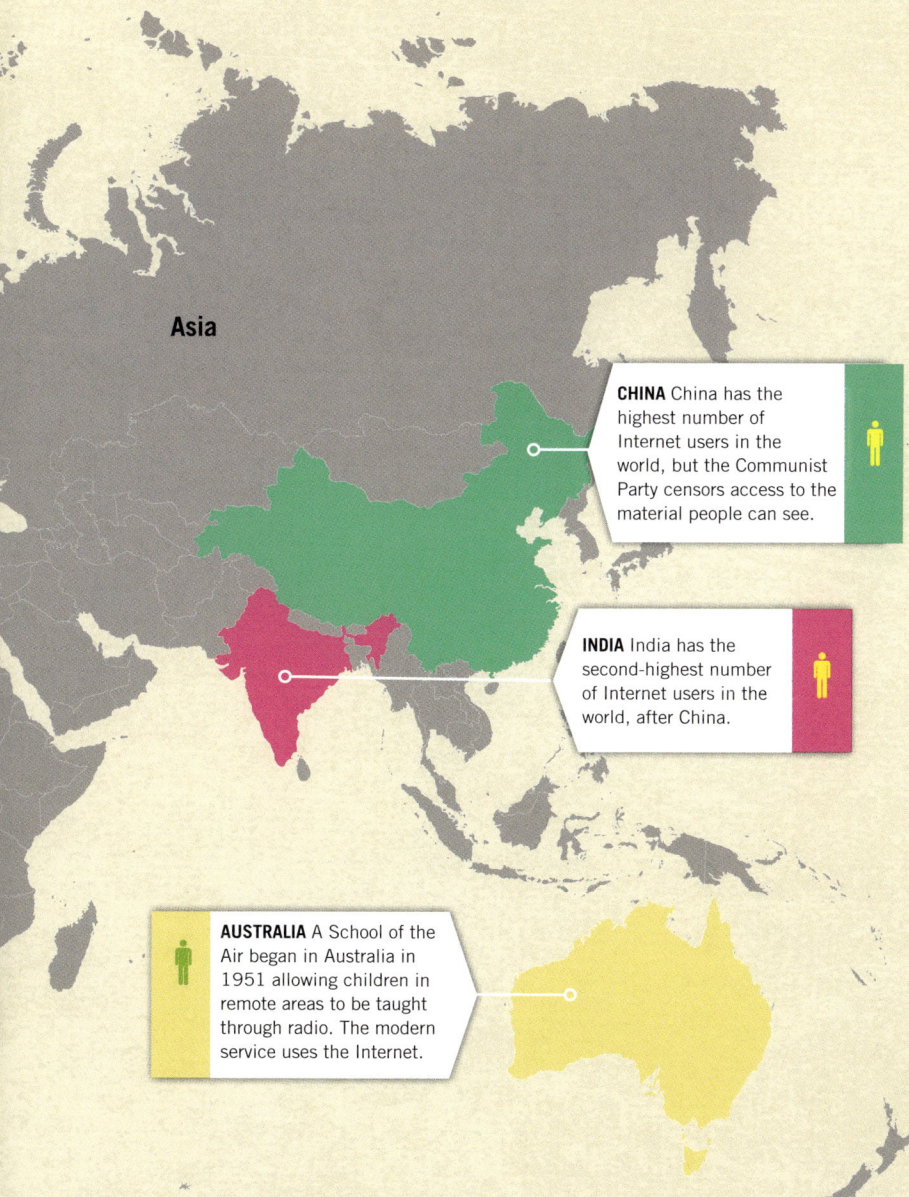

Asia

CHINA China has the highest number of Internet users in the world, but the Communist Party censors access to the material people can see.

INDIA India has the second-highest number of Internet users in the world, after China.

AUSTRALIA A School of the Air began in Australia in 1951 allowing children in remote areas to be taught through radio. The modern service uses the Internet.

FACT FILE:
COUNTRIES WITH THE LOWEST RATES OF **LITERACY** IN 2016:

South Sudan	27%
Afghanistan	28.1%
Burkino Faso	28.7%
Niger	28.7%
Mali	33.4%,
Chad	35.4%
Somali	37.8 %
Ethiopia	39%
Guinea	41%
Benin	42.4%
Sierra Leone	43.3%
Haiti	48.7%
Senegal	49.7%
The Gambia	51.1%
Bhutan	52.8%

FACT FILE:
COUNTRIES WITH THE HIGHEST PROPORTION OF **UNIVERSITY GRADUATES** IN 2015:

Canada	56%
United States	52%
Japan	50%
Germany	49%
Israel	48%
South Korea	47%
New Zealand	45%
United Kingdom	42%
Ireland	40 %
Australia	38%
Finland	36%
Belgium	34%

TIMELINE

ca. 12,000 BCE — Artists paint wild animals and hand prints on the walls of a cave in Altamira, Spain.

ca. 3200 BCE — The world's first writing system develops in Sumer in Mesopotamia. Other writing systems are independently developed shortly afterward in Egypt and India.

ca. 2590 BCE — Architects in Egypt have the math and engineering skill to build vast pyramids, and specialized workers to help bring their plans to reality.

ca. 500 BCE — The Chinese teacher Confucius argues that education and talent are more important for the government of the country than privilege and rank.

ca. 480 BCE — The city-state of Athens in Greece becomes the focus of a golden age of philosophy, math, natural science, and literary activity.

117 CE — The Roman Empire reaches its greatest extent. Roman settlement of Europe, North Africa, and the Middle East spreads Greek knowledge widely.

476 — Rome is overthrown by Germanic peoples, beginning a decline that later ages will call the Dark Ages.

800 — Charlemagne becomes Holy Roman Emperor. He encourages scholarship by setting up a school in Aachen. Learning is international because it is done in Latin, the language of ancient Rome.

ca. 1200 — Texts by classical writers such as Plato and Aristotle begin to reach Europe via the Islamic Middle East, where they have been preserved.

ca. 1300	The cultural movement known as the Renaissance begins in Europe. Europeans see the period as a rebirth of classical knowledge.
ca. 1440	In Germany, Johannes Gutenberg invents a printing press with reusable type, making it possible to print books much more quickly and cheaply.
1517	The authority of the Catholic Church is challenged in the Reformation by Protestant reformers who emphasize the importance of people reading the Bible for themselves.
1790s	Noah Webster publishes *Noah Webster's Speller*, which teaches children to read while also trying to give them basic lessons about citizenship.
1800	Prussia, a state in what is now Germany, introduces mass schooling to try to improve the quality of its army.
1880	Britain makes elementary schooling mandatory for all children aged between five and ten years.
1916	Albert Einstein publishes his theory of general relativity, a work that symbolizes the emergence of a new kind of science.
1945	The atom bomb, developed by a team of US and European physicists, is dropped on Japanese cities, forcing Japan to surrender and ending World War II.
1989	British scientist Tim Berners-Lee outlines his vision of the World Wide Web, in which information becomes easily shared by users with computers.
ca. 2010	The growth of social media and cloud technology broaden the ways in which knowledge is shared and the type of information people exchange.

GLOSSARY

academic Relating to education and scholarship.

Allies In World War II, the countries fighting Germany and Japan, including the United States, Great Britain, France, and the Soviet Union.

aqueducts Channels for moving water.

astronomers People who study the stars and other heavenly bodies.

bacteria Tiny organisms that cause infection and disease.

chemistry The study of the substances that make up matter.

classical Relating to the ancient civilizations of Greece and Rome.

colonies Areas settled and ruled by a country in another country.

curriculum The subjects covered by a course of study in a school.

empires Large groups of states ruled over by a single emperor or empress.

epics Long poems about the deeds of heroes or heroines from the past.

grammar The structure and correct use of a language.

illiterate Unable to read or write.

literacy The ability to read and write.

logic A way of reasoning according to strict rules about what is known.

morality Principles about what is right or wrong, or good or bad behavior.

nationalistic Believing that one's own country is superior to others.

philosopher A person who studies ideas about knowledge, truth, and the nature and meaning of life.

professional Related to traditional professions, such as medicine or the law.

rituals Religious ceremonies performed in a particular way.

scribes People who keep records in writing.

segregated Describes something that is set apart, or separated.

Sunday schools Schools that open on Sundays and are often linked to churches.

supernatural Not explained by the laws of nature.

theoretical Based on theory rather than practical knowledge.

theory An explanation of something based on ideas rather than known facts.

treatises Written works that explain a subject in a systematic way.

FURTHER RESOURCES

Books

Anderson, Jennifer Joline. *Albert Einstein.* Great Minds of Science. Minneapolis: Core Library, 2014.

Eliott, Lynne. *The Renaissance in Europe.* Renaissance World. New York: Crabtree Publishing Company, 2009.

Gow, Mary. *The Great Thinker: Aristotle and the Foundations of Science.* Great Minds of Ancient Science and Math. Berkeley Heights: Enslow Publishers, 2010.

Nardo, Don. *The Scientific Revolution.* World History Series. Detroit: Lucent Books, 2011.

Niver, Heather Moore. *Tim Berners-Lee: Inventor of the World Wide Web.* Computer Pioneers. New York: PowerKids Press, 2016.

Romanek, Trudee. *Science, Medicine, and Math in the Early Islamic World.* Life in the Early Islamic World. New York: Crabtree Publishing Company, 2012.

Websites

www.biography.com/people/johannes-gutenberg-9323828
This brief biography of Johannes Gutenberg explains the influence of his printing press.

http://www.ducksters.com/history/mesopotamia/sumerian_writing.php
This Ducksters.com page provides information about the invention of writing in Sumer.

http://www.ducksters.com/history/renaissance_science.php
This Ducksters.com page looks at some of the people who shaped the Scientific Revolution.

http://greece.mrdonn.org/philosophy.html
This page from Mr. Donn is an introduction to ancient Greek philosophy, with links to other pages.

http://www.historylearningsite.co.uk/medieval-england/medieval-education/
Learn how medieval children were educated on the History Learning Site.

http://people.howstuffworks.com/public-schools1.htm
The history of public education in the United States from How Stuff Works.

Publisher's note to educators and parents: Our editors have carefully reviewed these websites to ensure that they are suitable for students. Many websites change frequently, however, and we cannot guarantee that a site's future contents will continue to meet our high standards of quality and educational value. Be advised that students should be closely supervised whenever they access the Internet.

INDEX

A
African Americans 34
Age of Reason 29
Aristotle 13, 19, 23
astronomy 22, 28
atom bomb 37, 38, 39
Augustine, Saint 19

B
Berners-Lee, Tim 37, 41
Bible 18
Byzantine Empire 19, 22

C
Catholic Church 25, 28
cave painting 6
Charlemagne 19, 20
chemistry 29
Christianity 18–19
Cicero 15, 16
classical knowledge 20, 23, 24
communications 37, 40
computers 5, 40, 41
Confucius 13, 17
Copernicus, Nicolaus 28

D
Darwin, Charles 35
Diderot, Denis 29

E
education 22, 30–35
Egypt, ancient 4, 7, 8, 10
Einstein, Albert 36, 37, 38
electricity 35
evolution, theory of 35

F
Faraday, Michael 35
Fleming, Alexander 39

G
Galilei, Galileo 28
grammar schools 26
Greece, ancient 4, 12, 13, 14, 15, 17
Gutenberg, Johannes 24, 25, 26

H I L
Homer 12
humanism 24, 25, 26
Industrial Revolution 30
Islam 22–23
knowledge, definitions 6, 7, 14, 35, 41, 42
literacy 27, 33, 43

M N
madrasahs 23
medicine 39
Mesopotamia 7, 9
monasteries 18, 20, 21
moon landing 40
Newton, Isaac 28, 37

P Q
physics 37
Plato 13, 14, 19
printing press 5, 24, 26
Protestantism 26, 27
Pythagoras 13
Quran 22, 23

R
Raikes, Robert 32
Reformation 25, 26
religion 4, 5, 16–17
Renaissance 16, 24, 25
Rome, ancient 4, 13, 14, 15, 16, 17, 18, 19

S
scholasticism 19
schools 14, 16, 20, 21, 22, 23, 25, 26, 31, 32, 34
sciences 35, 37
scientific revolution 28–29
scribes 10, 11
Socrates 12, 13
space race 40
Sumer 10
Sunday schools 32

T U
technology 38, 40
"Three Rs" 32
towns 21, 22, 27
United States 33, 34, 38
universities 26, 27, 43

W
Washington, Booker T. 34
Webster, Noah 31, 33
World War I 38
World War II 38, 40
World Wide Web 5, 37, 39, 41
writing 4, 5, 7, 9, 10, 11, 20